UX DESIGN and USABILITY MENTOR BOOK

With Best Practice Business Analysis and User Interface Design
Tips and Techniques

From the Best Selling Author

EMRAH YAYICI

About the Author

Emrah Yayici is the author of best-selling *Business Analyst's Mentor Book*. He is one of the managing partners of UXservices, BA-Works and Keytorc. He started his career as a technology consultant at Arthur Andersen and Accenture. Afterward he led global enterprise transformation projects at Beko-Grundig Electronics.

During his career he has managed multinational and cross-functional project teams in banking, insurance, telecommunications, media, consumer electronics, and IT industries. He is now sharing his experience about user experience design, usability testing, business analysis and software testing by publishing articles and books and by speaking at conferences.

He contributes to UXPA (The User Experience Professionals Association) as a member and IIBA® (International Institute of Business Analysis) as a local chapter president. He also contributed to ISTQB® (International Software Testing Board) as a former international board member.

Preface

The motto of this book is: *building user interfaces around users.*

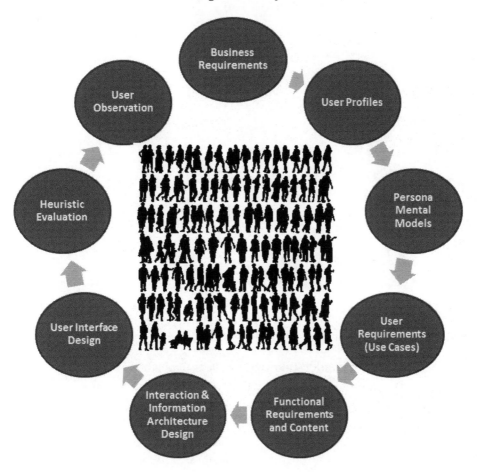

This can be achieved by applying a *user centered approach* that is a combination of best practice business analysis and UX design principles, tools, and techniques, including the following:

- Prototyping

- Usability testing techniques such as eye-tracking

- Lean product development with agile vs. waterfall

- Use cases

- User profiling

- Personas

- Interaction design

- Information architecture

- Content writing

- Card sorting

- Mind-mapping

- Wireframes

- Web page design guidelines

- Automation tools

- Customer experience evaluation

- Mobile UX design

The book includes real-life experiences and examples to help readers apply these best practices in their own organizations.

There is a common misunderstanding that user experience design is a matter of only *visual* user interface design; however a great user experience on a product can only be achieved if its user interfaces are not only visually aesthetic but also *functional and usable.*

This book is an extension of best-selling *Business Analyst's Mentor Book*. Thanks to the integrated business analysis and UX design methodology it presents, *UX Design and Usability Mentor Book* can be used as a guideline to create products that are both functional and usable.

Table of Contents

1. Define UX Design Roles and Responsibilities

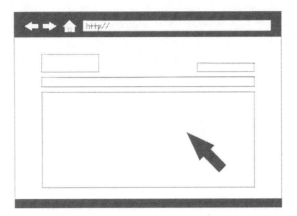

In many companies one of the most important challenges is designing the best UI (user interfaces) for their products.

To achieve this objective, companies should first shift their focus from designing the best UI to designing the best user experience (UX) for their products' users.

In the cases when design thinking is limited to the best UI, the focus is usually given only to visual aspects. But the best UX can be achieved only if usability is also positioned as a must-have throughout the analysis and design process in addition to functionality and visual aesthetic concerns. Usability is the criterion that determines how easy a product is for its users. Even if it is very elegant and has great functionality, a product cannot fully meet the needs of its users unless it is usable.

Companies that are willing to mitigate this risk set up dedicated UX teams to design the best experience for their users. A UX team includes the following roles:

1. *User researchers* do research and provide insight about user profiles and needs by applying techniques such as ethnographic research, persona definition, and mental modeling.

2. *Interaction designers* use requirement documents and user profiles as input to create prototypes of user interfaces by applying UX design and usability principles.

3. *Information architects* define content categories and navigation structures of user interfaces by using techniques such as mind-mapping and card-sorting.

4. *Usability testers* conduct heuristic evaluations and user observations to find product-usability problems.

Due to budget and resource limitations, these roles are combined in one single role, called *UX designer* in most organizations.

UX designers prepare prototypes and user interface annotation documents and send them to *visual designers*, who are in charge of creating visually aesthetic user interfaces.

These visual designs are then sent to *front-end developers* to be coded as the user interfaces of the product.

Business Analyst's UX Designer Role

In most companies the role of UX designers is totally played by business analysts whose own responsibility is mainly gathering requirements from clients and documenting them for the best understanding of developers.

Assignment of UX design role to business analysts may be due to budget constraints or lack of awareness on the importance of UX and usability at those companies. Under these circumstances, business analysts have to spend more time and effort to improve their knowledge and skills on these fields.

In large-scale organizations such as banks, there usually exits a separate UX design team. However, business analysts are still responsible for UX design of majority of the software products, because UX designers cannot afford to design and update thousands of user interfaces for hundreds of software products in these companies. In this case UX designers should focus on designing user interfaces of customer-facing products (such as Internet banking and mobile banking), and business analysts should be responsible for the design and update of enterprise software products' (such as core banking and accounting software) user interfaces that employees use.

The Secret of Creating Products That Provide Great User Experience

Whether it is the responsibility of business analysts or UX designers, the key success factors to ensure the best user experience on a company's products are the same:

1. Adaptation of UX design principles and guidelines in product development lifecycle

2. A design thinking based on business requirements

3. A user-centered requirements analysis and UX design methodology

4. A usability testing process that ensures an iterative product development lifecycle

5. Using requirements management, prototyping, and usability testing tools with a smart automation strategy.

In the following chapters, the book explains tools, techniques, and tips that should be implemented to realize each of these success factors.

2. Adapt UX Design and Usability Principles

Instead of searching for the best style sheets and design patterns, companies should first focus on adapting UX design principles in their user interface design process. Once adapted, these principles assure the usability of user interfaces designed in the company.

User experience design is a multidisciplinary field based on human computer interaction, computer science, ergonomics, and especially psychology.

The following well-known human-centered principles should be adapted in UX design process to ensure best experience for users:

- Simple Is Difficult!

The best user interfaces are simplistic and intuitive ones on which users can easily find what they are looking for and complete their tasks with minimum effort and error.

On the opposite side, busy and noisy interfaces make the experience complicated for users. This kind of designs can be easily created by distributing the functional specs randomly on different parts of user interfaces without too much design thinking.

However, it is not that easy to create simplistic and intuitive designs. Simplistic designs require extra time and effort. The secret to achieve simplicity in design is best explained in the quotation from famous novelist Antoine de Saint Exupery: "A designer knows he has achieved perfection not when there is nothing left to add, but when there is nothing left to take away."

In simplifying user interfaces, an Einstein quotation should also be remembered to prevent the risk of false simplicity: "Everything should be made as simple as possible, but not simpler." The unnecessary parts of the user interface should be removed to make the interface simpler, unless these parts clear away any product functionality.

- "Easy to Use" vs. "Easy to Learn"

Ideally user interfaces should be designed to be simple enough to leave no need for learning how to use the product.

Nevertheless, this is sometimes challenging for some products, such as task-intensive enterprise software used to manage internal company operations (such as accounting, human resources, and marketing software). In spite of all the efforts, it may be hard to simplify the interfaces of these enterprise applications. If user interfaces of these products are not "easy to use," then they should at least be "easy to learn." This can be achieved by designing interfaces in a consistent way. Consistency lets employees apply the knowledge they have gained while using one part of the product during their experience with the other parts. In case employees still have questions, user interfaces can guide them with contextual help menus and user manuals.

Also, there is a possibility of training employees on how to use this kind of software. By training employees, shortcomings for "easiness to use" can be compensated by "easiness to learn."

On the other side, it is not feasible to train all customers about how to use a company's software products. Thus, customer-facing applications should always have top-level usability.

- Focus Problem

People have difficulty in focusing on more than one object at the same time. During usability tests with the eye-tracking technique, this fact is always apparent. For instance, when an informative carousel image is displayed on the upper middle part of the interface, most users at least shoot a glance at it. However, when another image is located next to it, most users ignore both images and don't look at either one.

This fact necessitates selecting the highest priority content and design objects instead of displaying all of them on user interfaces at the same time.

- Consistency

Nowadays most companies aim to apply an omni-channel approach that allows users to start their experience in one interaction channel and continue it on another one.

For example, users booking a flight on a mobile application can buy the ticket on the web page and check in on a kiosk. People expect consistent menu structures, navigation flows, and call-to-actions on all of these interaction channels. Once they complete a task successfully at one channel, they expect to complete other tasks the same way on the other channels.

For example, if users once made a credit card payment under the Credit Cards menu of the ATM, they expect to also do it under the same menu item on mobile or web channels. If the payment option is placed under another menu, such as Payments, they experience difficulty in navigating to the right place.

- Bias Problem

Users have a bias towards evaluating new designs according to their similarity with the old design, and usually prefer the older one, which they are familiar with.

In usability tests when the users are asked to comment on the new design, they usually say, "The older one was better; I don't know why, but it was better!" Due to this fact, it is not wise to change the user interfaces too frequently if not really necessary. Besides, if possible, the new design should inherit the main design patterns of the old design that users are accustomed to.

- User vs. Designer Mental Model

Designers should not assume that users already know everything that they know and think the same way as they do.

For example, in most web-based products, the only way to navigate back to the home page is clicking on the brand's logo. However, in usability tests we see that the majority of novice users don't have an idea about this call-to-action. Therefore, another option should be provided for users to navigate back to the home page.

Similarly, in recent mobile applications, there is a popular feature called Send to Cloud that enables online saving of files to remote servers. During usability tests for a global mobile systems development company, our UXservices team observed that most novice users didn't understand the meaning of Cloud in this context, and they hesitated to use that feature. Some of the users even thought that Cloud was the name of a person on the contact list!

To prevent this kind of failure, interfaces should always speak the language of users and not of the designers.

- Pictures vs. Text

In ancient history people first started to draw pictures to communicate with one another before they invented the letters. Even Einstein said, "If I can't picture it, I can't understand it." In UX design, metaphors are used for this purpose.

Metaphors are visual figures that resemble an object or activity in real life. Using metaphors on interface designs is a very effective way of communicating the intended message and improving recognition. They make design ideas easier for users to understand. They are also easier to remember than text.

To improve usability, self-explanatory metaphors should be used. If users have difficulty in understanding the metaphor, then the metaphor should be used together with a title or brief description explaining what it represents.

Metaphors should also be kept simple. Users should not interpret extra meanings other than the metaphor's purpose of use.

- Gestalt Principles

People have a tendency to group items. According to gestalt principles, users form a natural grouping of items according to the items' proximity, symmetry, and similarity with one another. To achieve intuitive designs, gestalt principles should be applied for appropriate grouping and placement of design objects on user interfaces. Otherwise people make the wrong grouping of interface components, and this error condition misleads them during their interaction with the product.

In one of UXservices projects, the client asked our team to conduct user observation sessions on their Internet banking channel. The observed personas were all representing personal account owners. During the study our team observed that 10 percent of users locked their accounts while they were attempting to log in to their personal accounts. Although users were logging in with the correct account numbers and passwords, they were entering this information to the corporate account log-in section instead of the personal account log-in section. This was due to the wrong grouping of log-in sections on the main page. This usability defect was fixed by separating personal and corporate account log-in sections to a distance that users could easily distinguish.

- Context

Context is one of the most important factors that impacts human behavior in the usage of products.

"Context" is often confused with "content," but they are completely different concepts. Context's explanation in design is very similar to its meaning in archeology. For an archaeologist, context means the place where an artifact is found. The artifact itself (content) is not explanatory enough to make predictions about history. It should be evaluated together with the attributes of the place it is found.

Likewise, context in user interface design refers to the surrounding factors that influence the behavior and expectations of users.

This situation can be easily observed at companies such as banks where there are many alternative touch-points with customers. User behavior is different at each channel due to context. For example, while a live video chat feature is a good customer service solution for Internet banking users, it is not a good feature for ATM users, due to the negative reactions of impatient customers waiting in the queue.

- Cognitive Load

People fail to complete tasks in case their cognitive load reaches to a certain limit. This usually happens when their memory and perception level is forced.

To improve usability, minimize the cognitive load of users by using reminders, automatic computations, and other effort-minimizers on user interfaces.

- Need for Quick Help

People appreciate help mostly when it is provided at the moment it is really needed. They wish to find a solution to their problem as quickly as possible.

Thus instead of generic and loaded help documents, help about user interfaces should be provided in a contextual manner and address the specific problem of the user at the precise moment she needs it.

3. Adapt UX Design and Usability Guidelines

$$y'_u \quad y = u^2 + 3\sqrt{u} - 1 \quad u = x^4 + 1 \quad y'_x =;$$

$$' = (u^2 + 3\sqrt{u} - 1)'_u (x^4 + 1)'_x = (2u + u$$

$$\frac{3}{\sqrt{u}})^{*4x} \quad y'_x = (2x^4 + 2 + \frac{3}{2\sqrt{x^4} - 1})^{*4x};$$

$$_u (1 + \frac{2}{x})^{x+5} = ((1 + \frac{2}{x})^{\frac{x}{2}})^2 \cdot (1 + \frac{2}{x})^5 \; \lim_{x \to}$$

$$z^2 \cdot 1 = z^2 \quad \lim_{x \to a} \sqrt[p]{f(x)} = \sqrt[p]{\lim_{x \to a} f(x)}$$

$$A \lim b^{f(x)} = b^A, \; b = const, \; \lim_{x \to a} f(x) =$$

$$_a \log_c f(x) = \log_c [\lim f(x)], \; c = const \quad \lim_{x \to}$$

19

UX design principles remain valid and up-to-date for years, since they are mostly human-centered. But this fact is not true at the guideline level. As technology and social trends change, most of these guidelines lose their validity. The ones that are based on human behavior are exceptions, since the physiological and behavioral attributes of human beings remain the same. These kinds of guidelines are the best ones that can be used in building standard UX design templates such as style sheets and usability checklists. Some of these well-known UX design and usability guidelines are as follows:

- *Use colors to draw attention, to group items on user interfaces, to show status, and to get attention.*

For a minimalist and aesthetic design, limit the number of colors on the same user interface to five.

- *Provide feedback to users for situations such as*

> - wrong data entry;

> - long response time (highly recommended if users will have to wait for more than four seconds); and

> - needing user approval for further progress.

Balance the frequency of feedback given to users on user interfaces. Although it is informative, giving feedback too often (either by two-step interaction or dialogue) interrupts the user experience. In giving feedback, use professional and positive language that is not blaming users.

- *Be careful in using default values. Don't use them unless you are sure that they won't bring a risk of selecting wrong options.*

- *Use simple and to-the-point metaphors.*

Select metaphors that users are most familiar with. This is especially important when there is age diversity among users. For example, an old-style TV set or a wired phone may not be good metaphors for young users. Usage of mobile phone and flat screen TV images will be more appropriate in this case.

Balance usability with performance. Using too many metaphors may result in performance problems. Don't forget that the maximum tolerable waiting time for users is two seconds.

- Use shortcuts for expert users. Ask for approval of critical transactions such as adding, deleting, or modifying high-priority data.

- Users focus on faces the first time they look at a user interface. Don't use face visuals on low-priority areas of interest.

- Don't treat users as subscribers by requesting too much personal information at the beginning of an interaction with them.

For example, don't ask for detailed information for online membership to your website if that information is not really needed. If you need detailed user data for CRM (customer relationship management) purposes, then reward your users or at least tell them about the future benefits of providing accurate data (e.g., loyalty programs). Otherwise users fill in those fields randomly with incorrect data, and your database soon becomes garbage.

- Allow customization of user interfaces for expert users.

However, limit customization to a certain level to prevent complexity. According to Hick's law, increasing the number of choices increases the time for making a decision logarithmically.

- People divide information into chunks.

Thus group content such as menu items instead of listing them one under the other. In chunking content, remember that the ideal number of items in a group is four.

- People are impatient.

Make high-priority tasks and content highly visible. Users stop interaction if they can't find what they are looking for after four or more clicks.

- People judge products mostly based on their first impression.

Designers should build a good first impression on the main user interface and sustain it on the subsequent ones.

- People avoid looking at banner areas.

Prevent the risk of banner blindness by avoiding banner-like user interface components.

- Reduce busyness and complexity of user interfaces by using white spaces.

White spaces are also helpful in separating user interface components and chunks of information.

- Don't use radio buttons for more than five options. Instead use a select menu.

- Don't use abbreviations unless you are sure that the users know them.

However, if an abbreviation is more straightforward for users compared to what it represents, then keep using it.

This situation was witnessed at a bank. The bank changed the menu name from EFT (electronic funds transfer) to Money Transfer to Another Bank on their Internet banking interfaces. However, a considerable number of customers who were accustomed to the EFT menu label couldn't make money transfers and complained about this problem. The bank had to change the menu label back to EFT again.

- Include search functionality.

According to our experience at UXservices projects, more than 30–35 percent of people are search-oriented. For instance, instead of directly entering a website's URL on the browser, these users search for that website on search engines and navigate through the links listed on search results. Similarly this kind of user looks for a search box on any application to search for an item or function instead of navigating through the menus of the user interfaces.

However, in most applications, search functionality does not work as it's intended. Users cannot find some of the items or functions they are looking for, although they exist somewhere in the application. To prevent this failure, search boxes should not be used unless they work with high accuracy, like search engines do.

- Do not create memory workload on users.

Users should not be forced to remember the details of their interaction on previous user interfaces they have visited. The product should remind the users of the information that they need. For example, if a user got a discount code on an online shopping site, it should be automatically displayed in the checkout process, in case the user selects the option of paying with a discount code.

4. Adapt Mobile UX Design and Usability Principles

Mobile devices have penetrated our lives and completely mobilized our personal and business lives.

In our personal lives, we use mobile devices to navigate in traffic, shop online, play games, and for many other personal-use cases.

Mobile devices have also penetrated the business life and become the mainstream platform for many use cases: organizing meetings, updating and sharing documents, networking with other professionals, and much more.

Every day thousands of mobile websites and mobile apps are developed to meet these personal and business use cases. Unfortunately only some of them can be successful. The secret of developing successful mobile products is creating a user experience that completely matches the characteristics of mobility.

To achieve this, UX designers should avoid positioning mobile products as a smaller copy of PC versions. For years banks made this mistake and created a small mobile copy of Internet banking called WAP (wireless application protocol). Although they made a lot of investment in this mobile technology, it didn't pay off. Although their WAP channel was successful in terms of functionality, it completely lacked usability.

To prevent falling into this trap, differentiating factors between mobile and PC should always be considered, and the following user-centered guidelines should be applied during mobile UX design:

- Consider form factor (small screen) at every part of the design.

Compared to the design for PC applications, be more sensitive in prioritizing and selecting the tasks and content that will be included in the mobile product.

Instead of including full PC functionality, choose a subset of features that are most appropriate to mobile use such as

- fulfilling instant needs, such as

- paying bills or

- checking bank-account balance;

- completing impulse transactions, such as

- buying a book suggested by a friend or

- making reservation for a flight;

- getting quick info, such as checking

- traffic info,

- exchange rates, or

- score of the games.

Rather than directing users to other platforms, let them be able to complete these types of tasks that are already initiated on mobile devices.

- Remember that mobile experience is very open to interruption.

Enable users to continue their transaction without any need to start from the beginning in case they are interrupted by an incoming call, e-mail, SMS, or an interruption from their surrounding environment.

-Use accelerators, auto-complete, and default values for fast completion of mobile transactions with minimized text entry and selection.

- Don't ask users to register or log in if not really needed for security and privacy concerns.

If needed, allow registration with minimum data entry.

- Remember that users are more impatient on mobile devices.

Inform users about system status if they will be waiting for a while for completion of a transaction.

- In the design of mobile apps and sites benefit from social and contextual information readily available on the mobile device.

For example, instead of sending mass messages, a mobile coupon application can send coupon codes to its users when they are near restaurants that allow payment with coupons.

- Ensure the use of similar design elements for similar functionalities to make users easily get familiar with the mobile application or site.

Using widgets, metaphors, gestures, and CTAs (call to actions) similar to the conventions used on the mobile operating system improves ease of use and learning. For instance, if you are designing an Android application, it is better to use the same conventions for search, add, and move conventions that are already used in default Android applications such as calendar, e-mail, and chat.

- Use gestures that are natural and easily predictable by users.

- Consider the big-thumb problem in deciding on the size of buttons and other CTAs on touch-screen devices.

- Apply inverted pyramid method for content-intensive mobile user interfaces.

First present the summary of most critical information together with a visual object, and then start to present the details in descending level of importance. News magazines use this classic journalistic method very effectively on their mobile apps and sites.

5. Realize that User Interfaces Are "Visualized Requirements"

"Architecture Begins Where Engineering Ends" – Walter Gropius

In many organizations there is a wrong culture of focusing more on outputs (deliverables) than on outcomes (value). However "doing the right thing is always more important than doing the thing right." Hence the objective should not be creating products with fancy user interfaces, but creating products with user interfaces that best meet requirements.

To achieve this objective, design stage should always start following a *requirements engineering* stage.

Requirements in a Nutshell

User interfaces are the visualized form of requirements. Therefore, before starting to design user interfaces, business analysts and UX designers should have a good understanding of requirements. There are five main types of requirements:

1. Business Requirements

Answer *why* clients (either customers or business units) needed / requested a new product or an enhancement on the existing ones.

2. User Requirements

Answer *what* user needs/goals (*use cases*) the product should meet.

3. Functional Requirements

Answer *what* functionality the product should have in order to meet user requirements.

4. Nonfunctional Requirements and Business Rules

Answer *how* the product should work in terms of nonfunctional requirements and business rules. Nonfunctional requirements are quality attributes of a product, such as usability, performance, privacy, and security. Business rules are mainly the conditions, constraints, and formulas that determine how requirements will be handled by the user and the product.

5. System Requirements

Answer *technically how* the product will function in terms of inner technical dynamics.

Cooking Analogy

The quality of user interfaces totally depends on the quality of requirements. While it is possible to cook bad food from good ingredients, it is not possible to cook good food from bad ingredients.

Similarly, although it is possible to build poor-quality user interfaces with well-defined requirements, it is not possible to deliver high-quality user interfaces with poor requirements, even with the best visual designers and front-end developers.

Well-defined requirements can be assured if the following best practices are applied while gathering and documenting requirements:

- Gather requirements in a user-centered way at interviews, focus groups, and workshop meetings with clients (either customers or business units).

> - Invite not only managers but also experts / users of the products to the meetings.

> - If needed, use ice-breaking techniques at the beginning of meetings to help people start working together and collaborating (such as asking them to introduce themselves).

> - Take notes but do not record requirements-gathering meetings. Make participants feel that what happens in requirements-gathering meetings, stays in requirements-gathering meetings.

> - In case you have difficulty in gathering requirements from clients, benefit from early prototyping by sketching user interfaces during the meetings.

> Use prototypes as a liaison between the client and yourself for requirements elicitation.

> - Don't make assumptions and provide early solutions. First, understand AS IS and then discuss TO BE.

> - Listen more and talk less during requirements-gathering sessions.

> - Don't be afraid to ask questions when something is not clear.

- In requirements-gathering meetings, giving right answers to wrong questions is worse than giving wrong answers to right questions. Wrong questions mislead the team, generate conflicts, waste project time, and generally result in failure. Prepare simple, objective, and to-the-point questions before these meetings. Get ready for the meetings by analyzing the existing product's user interfaces and documentation beforehand.

- The way of asking questions in requirements-gathering meetings is also important. The "observer effect" in quantum mechanics states that "by the act of watching, the observer affects the observed reality." Similarly, asking questions in a biased way impacts the objectivity of answers from clients during requirements-gathering meetings.

- Clients want the best solution that will help them achieve their goals in the easiest and fastest way.

Hence, during requirements-gathering meetings, highest priority should be given to translating business needs into correct user requirements. The conflicts on these requirements should be resolved before discussing the technical or design aspects of the system.

- Be Careful with Yes-Men

Arthur Schopenhauer said, "Every truth passes through three stages before it is recognized. In the first it is ridiculed, in the second it is opposed, in the third it is regarded as self-evident."

Business analysts and UX designers should not personalize the negative comments of participants who object to the proposed solutions throughout the meetings. Analysts and designers should get ready to deal with both "yes-men" and "no-men".

Yes-men are more dangerous than no-men. They are silent and friendly during requirements-gathering meetings but become aggressive and extremely demanding later, at user-acceptance tests.

Although no-men are usually regarded as troublemakers, they are more helpful in identifying conflicts in the early stages of the project.

Conflicts between participants should be considered positively during the requirements gathering meetings. Business analysts and UX designers should try to clarify and resolve all conflicts during the meetings. They should not postpone conflicts by entering them into an issue database. If these conflicts are not discussed and resolved at this early stage of the project, they will later appear as high-cost CRs (change requests) at UI design, development, and testing phases.

- Ask Why the Conflict Exists

As it is mentioned by Nobel Prize–winner Tinbergen, "There is no white or black in life; there are different tones of gray." Similarly, it is usually hard to create an exact win-win situation during the projects. However, it is still the most constructive and effective way of resolving conflicts.

The first rule of creating win-win situations is asking, "Why does the conflict exist?" Then both parties in the negotiation have to ignore their personal egos, behave objectively, and be empathic to find the answer to this question and move forward.

- Think Outside the Box

Albert Einstein said, "The problems that exist in the world now cannot be solved by the level of thinking that created them." To resolve conflicts about requirements and user interfaces, business analysts and UX designers should make paradigm shifts and approach problems from different perspectives.

For example, the ultrasonography technique, which is used for visualizing subcutaneous body structures by using sound waves, was discovered with a similar approach. Although sound waves were normally used in aural technologies, this time they were used for ophthalmic technologies. Like radars, this technology was also inspired by bats. A bat emits sound waves and listens to the echoes returning back to determine how far an object is, where it is, how big it is, and where it is moving. Similarly business analysts and UX designers should be open-minded, find alternative solution options, and prevent shallow "either/or" discussions with other project stakeholders in order to be able to resolve conflicts during requirements-gathering sessions.

In one of our UXservices mobile banking projects, the proposed solution included a feature that allowed users to search and display ATMs (automated teller machine) nearest to their location on a map. Client requested that if an ATM was out of order, this information should be shown as a note on the map. However, our UX designers mentioned that this was a rare case, and, in order to keep mobile user interfaces simpler, they didn't want to add this extra information.

After long and shallow either/or discussions on this issue, a business analyst proposed an alternative solution: "ATMs that were out of order at that time should not be even displayed on the map." This suggestion was evaluated to be technically feasible by developers and accepted by both client and the design team. Thinking outside the box is an important skill for business analysts and UX designers to resolve this kind of conflicts.

- Don't Exaggerate Problems

"It is not that I am so smart, it is just that I stay with problems longer," said Albert Einstein. Sometimes business analysts and UX designers feel desperate during requirements-gathering meetings, especially when the number of conflicts increases and the problems get complicated. At those times, they should remember that they are not doing rocket science like in NASA or CERN and should not exaggerate these situations.

Instead of giving up early, they should remember the advice of Henry Ford: "There are no big problems; there are just a lot of little problems." They should divide problems into smaller pieces and resolve them with a bottom-up approach.

- "The Closer You Look, the Less You See"

The key success factor in requirements analysis and UX design is the ability to prevent scope creep, which is the number one reason for project failures. Business analysts and UX designers should have the ability to see the big picture and have a holistic view of the requirements to best manage the product scope. As it was said at the opening stage of the movie *Now You See Me*, "The closer you look, the less you see."

- Good, Fast, Cheap Dilemma

Clients always want to get the best solution in shortest time with minimum cost. According to the Project Management Triangle, in a project you can only achieve two out of the three objectives of *good, fast*, and *cheap*.

It is almost impossible to achieve three of them at the same time. To produce a good product in a very short time will require a lot of high-quality resources and will not be cheap. To produce a high-quality product at minimum cost will take a considerable amount of time. And a product that is built in a short time with minimum cost will most probably not be a high-quality one.

At requirements-gathering meetings, clients should be informed and convinced about these trade-offs.

- Fair Value Principle

When time to market is the most important criterion, the project should be classified as a fast-track one. In these time-sensitive fast track projects, business analysts and UX designers should convince clients to get "fair value" outcomes with "must-have" features rather than many "nice-to-have" ones.

- Perfect Is the Enemy of Good

In requirements-gathering meetings, all kinds of specs and design ideas—including crazy and nice-to-have ones—should be articulated. However, when clients insist too much on these nice-to-have specs and design ideas, business analysts and UX designers should remind clients of the famous phrase in Voltaire's poem "La Begueule": "perfect is the enemy of good." The statement tells that insisting on perfection often results in no improvement at all.

In spite of all of these efforts, even in time-sensitive fast-track projects, clients are usually biased to expand the scope of the solution by adding nice-to-have features. In this kind of situations they should be reminded that "a bird in the hand is worth two in the bush". In the mobile banking project that was mentioned before, in spite of the tough project schedule, a manager of the client insisted that the mobile user interfaces should also display the number of people waiting in ATM queues. Our UXservices project team convinced him to keep this feature out of scope by explaining the risk of not being able to complete the project on time due to this kind of nice-to-have features.

- Priority Quadrant

Having a formal prioritization process is one of the maturity-level indicators of a company's requirements-management process.

In the lack of a prioritization process, clients feel free to request any feature, as if there are unlimited resources. The clients with the highest political power in the company usually get first places in the queue.

The features requested by clients should be prioritized according to two main criteria: business value and implementation difficulty.

Business value depends on alignment to business requirements. The items with high business value and low implementation difficulty should be rated as high priority, while the ones with low business value and high implementation difficulty should be rated as low priority. The rest of the features should be labeled as medium priority and prioritized according to their expected frequency of use and time-to-market constraints.

Medium-priority features should be relabeled as high priority if they have high frequency of use and there is enough time to implement them. Otherwise they should move to the low-priority quadrant.

- Next-Release Lie

When clients insist on nice-to-have specs and design ideas that are hard to develop, business analysts and UX designers sometimes get rid of these demands by postponing their requests. They say that this demand will be handled in the next release, although it will not!

However, promises are hard to forget. When the so-called feature is not developed in the next release, it damages the relationship between the client and the project team. Business analysts and UX designers should resolve these conflicts with the help of negotiation and communication skills instead of using this unethical, tricky way.

- Gold Plating

Business analysts should align the detail level of requirements documents to project needs and conditions.

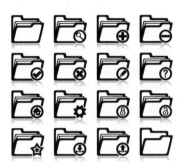

If the detail level of documents is too low, there is a risk of an incomplete requirements definition. In this case UX designers and developers have to guess about product features. They produce user interfaces that miss critical requirements, and this triggers a vicious cycle of CRs (change requests) in the future. And sometimes UX designers and developers add extra features on user interfaces that are not included in requirements documents by thinking that clients will be delighted to see them. This situation is called *gold plating*. Both CRs and gold plating are factors that result in scope creep during the projects.

- Consider Future Modification and Enhancement Needs

Business analysts and UX designers should aim to create user interfaces that can be easily modified when needed in the future. Otherwise clients' future enhancement and modification requests on the product will necessitate a huge amount of development effort on user interfaces. By time the total cost of ownership for existing products will reach a very high amount. This will create a weird situation, such as buying a cheap car whose final cost exceeds an expensive car due to the extra accessories added by time.

In one of CRM projects for a telecommunications company, our UXservices team used a combo box that enabled selection of the customer segment on the campaign definition form. But the developer proposed that using an option box would be technically easier for him.

UXservices business analysts suggested that the developer could easily create an updatable combo box by using web services. This would prevent the need for changing the form for each additional customer segment. The developer also agreed and moved forward with this more appropriate design. By this way unnecessary future effort that would be needed for each new customer segment addition was prevented.

- Keep Requirement Documents Updated for Future User Interface Changes

Requirement documents should be kept updated by business analysts even after the project. They should serve as a *reusable repository of requirements* when needed during future modifications on user interfaces. This will save a lot of time for the analysis and design team if clients request changes on user interfaces in the future.

Business analysts and UX designers can use traceability matrices to track which user interfaces will be impacted as a result of changes on requirements and business rules.

6. Base the Design Thinking on Business Requirements

If the First Button in a Shirt Is Put Wrong, Then Every Button Will Be Wrong

Business requirements define the value proposition of a product. They are the answers to *why* a new product is requested. For example, business requirements for an online apparel shopping site can be defined as

- being recognized as the best discount place for fashion products,

- being a trend-setter portal for fashion enthusiasts, and

- providing the best loyalty campaigns for members.

A clear definition of these business requirements at the start of the project is very important because all user, functional, nonfunctional, technical requirements, and business rules of the product should be defined in consistency with them. Wrong definition of business requirements has an adverse rippling effect on all of these low-level requirements of the product.

As the visualized form of requirements, user interface designs should be also based on business requirements to satisfy the strategic level objectives of creating that product. UX designers should initiate design process by reading and understanding documents that define business requirements.

Depending on the size of the project, business requirements can be found on different types of requirement documents.

Business Case Document

At large-scale projects that last six months or more, business requirements are documented on a business-case document. The business-case document also includes major features of the proposed solution and its benefits, costs, risks, and financial return indicators.

Vision and Scope Document

For medium- and small-sized projects that last between one and six months, business requirements are documented on a vision and scope document. This document also includes the features of the proposed solution that will be delivered in each release.

SOW (Statement of Work) Document

For enhancement/modification requests on existing products that last less than one month, there is usually no need for a business case or vision and scope document. Most of the time, a clear explanation of the business need in a one-page SOW document is enough to describe the scope of work. These requests are better fulfilled by a more agile approach in collaboration with client, without too much documentation.

Business Requirements Prevent CRs on User Interfaces

Clear definition of business requirements optimizes UX design process by steering every project stakeholder at the same strategic direction. Throughout the project, it mitigates the risk of scope creep due to potential CRs on user interfaces.

In one of our UXservices projects, client was trying to push a huge amount of specs into the design of a mobile banking application. But if all of these specs were included in the design, then the mobile app would be a miniaturized version of an Internet banking channel and would be very crowded and unusable.

In this project our UXservices analysis and design team was very lucky, because there was a business requirement on the vision and scope document indicating that "mobile banking application should satisfy only *instant* banking transaction needs of the customers," such as

- checking deposit account balance,

- transferring money,

- making a credit card payment,

- making a bill payment, and

- finding ATMS and branches at a specific location.

During the project, business analysts could easily cross-check the alignment of client requests against this high-priority business requirement and reject irrelevant requests without too much discussion. For example, a change request that asked for "including long-term loan and investment products on mobile user interfaces" was rejected without any conflict, since these long-term products were not related to instant banking needs. This clear business requirement prevented many similar change requests that would result in time-consuming changes on user interface designs.

7. Inspire from Gaudi and Steve Jobs's Way of User-Centricity

As mentioned in the previous chapter, business requirements set the strategic direction in any product development project. This makes the alignment of a product's user interfaces to its business requirements the most important success factor in UX design.

User-Centricity

The second most important success factor in UX design is *user-centricity*.

User interface design is like football. Everybody in the company feels confident and keen to comment on the designs. Upper management also loves to intervene in the design process by requesting last-minute changes, even on colors and page layouts on the eve of the product release.

Overcoming this challenge and designing user interfaces in a professional way requires a UX design approach that positions the users at the center. However, positioning users at the center does not mean doing everything according to their will. UX design approach should focus on identifying users' real needs, but at the same time it should promote innovation during design thinking. This fact is best summarized in Henry Ford's famous quotation: "If I had asked people what they wanted, they would have said faster horses."

In recent years companies have started to heavily invest in user/customer-centric methodologies. This is a logical investment, because nowadays competitors can quickly copy your company's products and services, but it takes a considerable amount of time for them to copy your user/customer-centric approach.

Banking is one of the industries where this situation is best witnessed. Today almost every bank has the same portfolio of commoditized products and services. And competing with low-price commissions and interest rates is not sustainable for them. The only way to gain competitive advantage is to be customer-centric by providing the best experience on all customer interaction channels, especially the self-service ones.

Previously the digital self-service channels of banks used to be regarded as an "alternative" to their branches. The only mission of these digital channels was to decrease costs by providing more efficiency. With increased penetration of broadband Internet connection and mobile devices, these alternative channels became the mainstream channels, proposing maximum customer value.

As a result, financial institutions had to be more user/customer-centric and started to redesign their ATM, web, and mobile-banking applications to improve their usability.

Gaudi's Organic Design Perspective

This evolution of user-centricity has been viable not only in finance but also in every industry. Throughout construction history, Gaudi has been the most famous architect, with his user-centered architecture design approach. His story starts with a childhood in which he suffered from poor health. This situation prevented him from going to school, and he spent most of his time in nature. His observations of nature inspired his design approach, which can be summarized as follows: "The great book always open and which we should make an effort to read, is that of Nature." With this philosophy he designed buildings with "organic style," which then became an important standard in architecture.

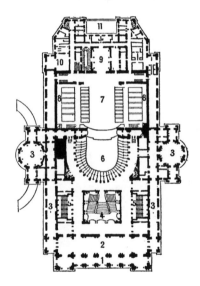

Natural-Born Users

Another man revolutionized the high-tech industry in a similar way. By positioning users at the center of the analysis and design process, Steve Jobs led the innovation of the most usable consumer electronics products ever.

He worked to create natural-born users of his products. Even kids could use his company's phones and touchpads with gestures similar to their natural behavior. This new design approach made his company one of the best performers in the high-tech industry.

After the success of this approach, it was realized that the humanization of products is not necessarily achieved by anthropomorphic features providing human like behavior. Rather it could be achieved by ensuring usability of products with a user centered design approach.

For instance a car cockpit design that allows easy navigation to the most used control buttons may be more usable than a car that can interact with its driver by voice recognition, control and feedback.

8. Adapt a User-Centered Business Analysis and UX Design Methodology

In product development Gaudi's and Steve Jobs's human-centered design philosophy can be implemented by applying a user-centered analysis and design approach in which *user interfaces are driven by user profiles and user requirements*. Below the methodology to implement this approach is explained step by step with an example: *UX Design of an apparel shopping web site*.

A. Identify User Profiles

"Designing for everybody" is not a feasible and effective strategy in terms of usability. Interfaces of a product are usable if they are good fit for its users. Thus user interface design should be based on the profile of target user groups.

Profiling can be done based on diverse user characteristics. For instance, users of an apparel shopping web site can be profiled according to their characteristics, such as

- age,

- gender,

- education,

- computer use comfort level,

- smart phone comfort level,

- social media comfort level, and

- business background.

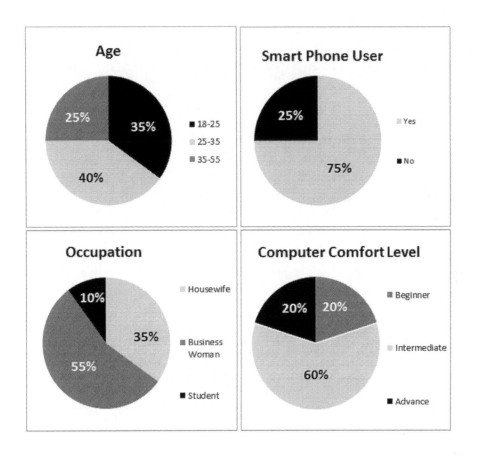

UX designers can define user profiles at requirements-gathering meetings facilitated by business analysts. An effective way to understand user profiles during requirements-gathering sessions is to ask users their opinions about the existing products. Users' comments about the existing products can be interpreted to understand users' own capabilities and weaknesses. This reminds us of a quotation of the famous philosopher Spinoza: "If Pierre tells something about Paul, we learn more about Pierre than we learn about Paul."

In addition to attending requirements-gathering meetings, UX designers should also conduct field-analysis techniques—such as job shadowing and user task analysis—to observe users in their own context and profile them accordingly.

B. Define Personas

Another important aspect of user-centricity is emotional design. Human beings judge things based on their left brains' logical and right brains' emotional capabilities. And most of the time, emotion is the main criterion in their judgments.

In alignment with their emotions, users first create a mental model of the products they use. This model guides them throughout their whole experience with the product. Therefore user interface designs should be based on mental model of users rather than of designers.

Personas, which are representative imaginary characters, are the best way to define the mental models of diverse user profiles and predict their expected behavior on user interfaces. Although there can be several user profiles for a product, UX designers should limit the number of personas at three (at most at four, in extreme cases) to prevent falling into the trap of "designing for everybody." A persona description should include a name, photo, demographic info, and a scenario section.

The personas for apparel shopping web site can be defined as follows:

Persona:1

"I have a very busy life"

July

As a banker business is the center of my life. I am working very hard during the week and mostly on Saturdays.

I love shopping. But I don't want to spend my only free time on Sunday for shopping. I rather prefer to spend my time for my family.

Thus online shopping is a must have rather than a nice to have activity for me.

Age: 29
Occupation: Business Woman
Income: > $ 100.000
Marital Status: Married
Interests: Travelling, Book Reading
Technical Profile: Comfortable with computer, smart phone user
Smart Phone User: Yes

I usually check the new arrivals and best sellers categories of the sites. I have no time to collect and use gift coupons or discount codes. However I sometimes check seasonal and sale promotions.

Persona: 2

"Shopping is my hobby"

Angela

My kids leave the home at 8:00 am and come back at 15:00 pm from the school. I have enough time for my hobbies during the day.

Age: 35

Occupation: Housewife

Income: < $ 50.000

Marital Status: Married

Interests: Shopping, fashion, decoration

Technical Profile: Beginner level computer skills

Smart Phone User: No

I love watching fashion channels and visiting online apparel stores to see the most trendy clothes, bags, shoes and accessories. By checking the bestsellers on online stores it is possible to see the most popular brands and items of the season.

It is also easier to track promotions on these sites.

But some of the online stores are really hard to use. Last time I found a very nice skirt at a very good price on one of these sites but I couldn't manage to purchase it with my discount code although I tried hard.

C. Define User Requirements (Use Cases)

Following user profiling and persona definitions, user requirements for the product are gathered.

In traditional business analysis approach, user requirements are gathered by asking the following question:

- Which features should the new product have?

The major drawback of this approach is a huge number of change requests during the project and many product features that are not used at all. The main reason for this drawback is the lack of user-centricity in this traditional product-centric approach.

A more user-centric analysis can be achieved by applying the *use case technique*. In use case–driven analysis, user requirements are gathered by asking the same question above in a different way in three steps:

1. Who are the actors?

User profiles and personas are used as an input to define actors of the product at this stage. An actor may represent two or more personas.

For the apparel shopping web site example, housewife and businesswoman personas are different representations of the same "customer" actor.

2. What are the goals (use cases) of actors in using the product?

User requirements (use cases) correspond to goals of actors in using the product. Mental models of personas are considered as an input during use-case definitions. Use cases are shown on a use-case diagram, which also represents the high-level scope of the product. The use-case diagram for apparel shopping web site can be as follows:

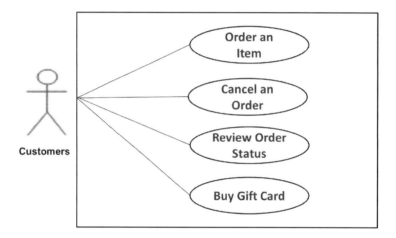

3. How will the actors interact with the product to achieve their goals?

A use-case document is prepared for each use case on the use-case diagram.

For the apparel shopping web site example, "Order an Item" use case can be documented as follows:

Use Case ID	01
Use Case Name	Order an item
Actors	Customer
Description	Customer searches, finds, orders, and pays for an item.
Preconditions	Customer logs in to the system using membership ID and password.
Postconditions	Order confirmation report is sent to the user via e-mail.
Main Scenario	1. User selects the category (jeans, skirts, accessories, etc.). 2. Under that category, user views the displayed items listed based on price and/or size. 3. User selects a particular item. 4. User reviews the details of the selected item and adds it in the shopping list. 5. User reviews the details on shopping list (description, color, size, availability, and price) for accuracy. 6. User controls the total amount of the shopping list. 7. User selects shipping type. 8. User enters payment and delivery data. 9. User confirms the payment. 10. User views "order confirmation report."
Alternative Scenario	1.1. User enters relevant product info in "search" instead of filtering (by size or price). 1.2. User views search results and selects the item she is looking for. 1.3. Back to Main Scenario—step 4.
Exception Scenario	7.1 If user selects fast delivery, she is notified with a message indicating that a commission rate will be charged for express deliveries (BR1).
Nonfunctional Requirements	NFR 1. Performance: After the request is submitted, search results should be listed within two seconds. NFR 2. Usability: If the billing address is same as the delivery address, user does not have to enter the same data twice.
Business Rules	BR1: Express Delivery Commission = 5 percent
Assumptions	Stock data received from the inventory system is up-to-date and accurate.

In use-case documentation, the following best practices should be considered:

- Describe interactions of actors with the product by use-case scenarios on the use-case document. Scenario steps (activities) correspond to functional requirements of the product.

While applying the use-case technique, there may be confusion about the difference between use case and functional requirement. Actually it is quite simple. Each use case represents a particular goal of an actor, whereas the activities to achieve that goal are functional requirements.

Let's explain this relationship with an analogy: If a bottle is considered as a product, "drinking water" is a use case, since it is a goal of an actor in using the bottle. But "opening the bottle cap" is not a use case, because it is not a particular goal of the actor. People don't buy bottles to open and close their caps. Opening the bottle cap is just a functional requirement to reach the goal of "drinking water."

Similarly "Order an Item" is a use case for the apparel shopping web site example, whereas "category selection" is one of the several functional requirements to achieve that specific use case.

- Separate main, alternative, and exception scenarios of the use case.

The main scenario represents the positive flow (happy path) of activities to achieve the goal of the actor in normal conditions.

Alternative scenarios define other possible ways of achieving the same goal.

Exception scenarios define the interaction of user and the product in error conditions.

For the "Order an Item" use case in apparel shopping web site example, if finding an item by filtering (by size or price) is described in the main scenario, then the discrete activities needed to find that item by using the "Search" functionality should be defined within an alternative scenario. The interaction between the user and the product (web site), in case the user attempts to order an item that is out of stock, should be defined as an exception scenario.

- Define exception scenarios separately from alternative scenarios.

Alternative scenarios may include some nice-to-have conditions that can be postponed until future releases, in case there is latency in the project. However, exception scenarios include error conditions, and they have to be implemented in any case.

- Use case documents aim to answer **what** *(functionality the product should have in order to meet user requirements) and* **how** *(the product should work in terms of nonfunctional requirements and business rules) questions.*

Clarifying the *technically how* (how the product will function in terms of inner technical dynamics) question is not a use case document's objective. Therefore don't include technical details on use-case documents.

- Define use-case scenarios with users' point of view, but don't include user interface details on them. User-interface details are defined later on prototypes and user-interface annotations based on use-case scenario definitions.

For example, "user filters items from drop-down menus located on the upper left part of the screen" is a wrong scenario activity definition. "User filters the items (by size or price)" is just enough.

- In addition to functional requirements also define nonfunctional requirements, business rules, and assumptions on use-case documents.

- Define business rules in a parametric way.

This will let the project team easily design, code, and change business rules when needed.

For example, in the "Order an Item" use case, "User is notified with a message indicating that 5 percent commission will be charged for express deliveries" is a wrong functional requirement definition. Instead it should be defined as "User is notified with a message indicating that a commission rate will be charged for express deliveries (BR1)." Business rules in this scenario should be defined at the business-rules section of the same use-case document. The business rule in this example should be defined as follows:

BR1: Express Delivery Commission = 5 percent

- Define nonfunctional requirements such as usability, performance, and privacy for each use case in a verifiable (testable) way.

For example, "Search results should be listed fast" is not a correct performance requirement definition. It should be defined as "After the request is submitted, the search results for items should be listed within two seconds."

- Limit assumptions to the conditions on which the user or product has no control.

For example, "the accuracy of stock data received from the inventory system" may be an assumption for the "Order an Item" use case. But, "all the items that may be ordered by customer are in stock" is not a correct assumption. The behavior of the customer and the product (apparel shopping web site), in the case of the user attempting to order an out-of-stock item, should be defined as an exception scenario on the use-case document.

- Benefit from flow charts to visualize use-case scenarios.

In history, people first used drawings to communicate with one another. Even after the invention of letters, they continued to use drawings as an easy way of expressing themselves. Similarly, using diagrams such as flow charts is an effective way of visualizing use-case scenarios and clarifying the ambiguities in narrative requirement definitions on plain-text use-case documents.

Flow charts are similar to activity diagrams in UML (unified modeling language). They are useful for modeling and describing work-flows with simple diagramming conventions. A flow chart is created for each use case. Each branch on a flow chart represents either the main, alternative, or exception scenario of a use case.

The flow chart below represents an "Order an Item" use case of the apparel shopping web site example. The branches on the chart show the main, alternative, and exception scenarios of that specific use case.

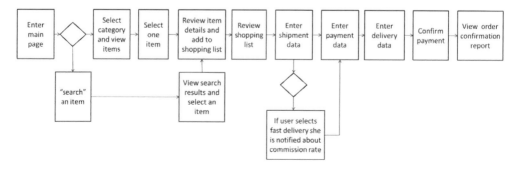

D. Interaction Design

At this step interaction between the user and the product is designed. If well defined, use cases and flow charts form a perfect basis for interaction design. During interaction design boxes on the branches of the flow chart are grouped within containers. These containers (dashed boxes) become a primary user-interface window, a dialogue box, or a message box. Or several containers combine and form a single user interface. Links between flow chart containers become navigation elements, such as links. This method mitigates the risk of missing any functionality on user interfaces. It also prevents the mismatch between the flow of use-case scenarios and the flow of user interfaces, which should normally be parallel to ensure usability.

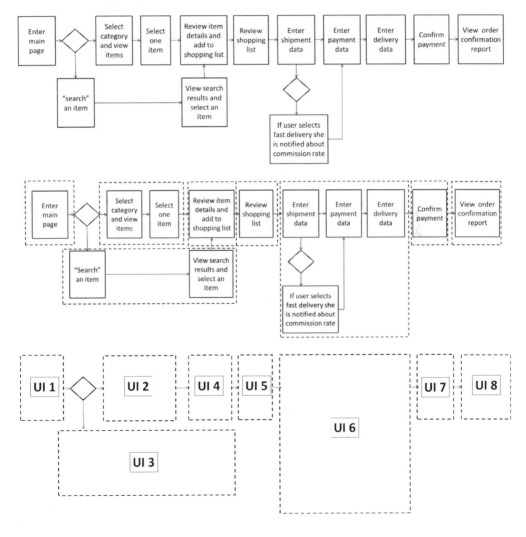

E. Information Architecture

User interfaces are composed not only of functional requirements (tasks) but also of content requirements.

Therefore, in parallel to interaction design (based on functional requirements), the information architecture (based on content requirements) should be also designed.

The main objective of information architecture design is to identify content requirements, define content categories, and finalize the navigation structures.

During information architecture design, the following techniques can be applied:

- Mind-Mapping

Mind-mapping is a popular technique that is used to identify content requirements.

By considering each persona's expected behavior on user interfaces, their mental model is mind-mapped. In this way the high-priority content requirements for each persona are identified.

In the apparel shopping web site example, the mental model of July (businesswoman) and Angela (housewife) personas can be mind-mapped as follows to identify their high-priority content requirements.

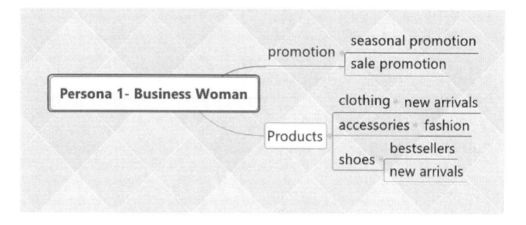

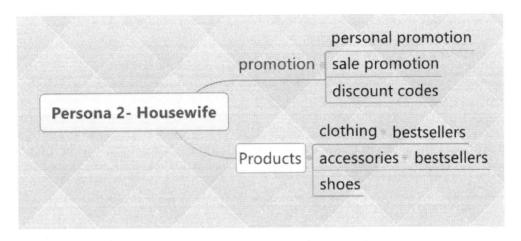

Based on content requirements, detailed content is written. At this stage the content writer should be also user-centered and consider the following attributes of best practice content:

- Concise

- Have sentences and paragraphs that are short and to the point.

- Leave no room for misinterpretation.

- Do not include flowery language with unnecessary adjectives such as "state of the art" "robust," "ideal," "unique," and "optimized."

- Include everything users need and nothing they don't:

Have content that is simple and expressed with a minimum number of words. Mark Twain's quotation describes this situation very well: "I didn't have time to write a short letter, so I wrote a long one instead." This simplistic approach in content writing has also been the differentiating success factor for Twitter in replacing classical blog sites.

- Useful

- Rather than offering a one-size-fits-all approach, the content should address the information needs of the target personas. Persona representatives should feel that the content is especially created for them.

Content should help users make a decision regarding solutions to their specific problems. It should have clear links and CTAs to the parts of user interfaces that present these solutions.

- Sharable

- Present key content in a way that users can easily share it with other users through social media, blog posts, e-mail, or other communication channels.

For web pages and mobile applications, sharable content creates a viral impact, thanks to evangelists of your products and services. Evangelists are the best users who create new users of your products.

- Reachable

SEO (search engine optimization) performance should be also considered in creation of the content for web-based products. Search engines have long been the main gateway for users to reach companies' products and services.

The most common keywords and phrases that users selected when searching for solutions to their similar needs should be identified and made the backbone of the content.

- Updated

Social media is also called real-time media, and that is what made it a very popular communication channel. As a take-away lesson from this success story, the content of web and mobile applications should be as dynamic and up-to-date as possible.

This can be achieved by using active CMS (content management systems), integrated blogs, and social media. By allowing review, ratings, and comments, this open communication platform enables two-way communications with users.

- Positive

A good user experience cannot be built on content that has negative wording.

Even error messages should not blame users. Instead they should direct them to the correct action in a positive tone.

- Consistent

The tone of the content should be consistent throughout the whole experience. It is better to use an honest tone throughout all user interfaces.

- Card-Sorting

Menu is one of the mostly used navigation tools to group and display the content on user interfaces. If content is not grouped under correct menu labels, users have difficulty in finding what they are looking for. This is a very common type of usability defect.

Card-sorting is an effective information architecture technique to prevent this risk. It is used for categorization of content that will be listed under menus or other navigation objects. In card-sorting technique, menu items are written on cards, and users that represent personas are asked to group these items under correct menu labels. There are two types of card-sorting techniques. In *closed card-sorting*, menu labels are already determined. Users are only asked to sort a series of cards representing menu items under the most appropriate menu label. In *open card-sorting*, users define the menu labels themselves and group menu items under these labels. These natural groupings created by the card-sorting technique are then used to formulate navigation structures. For example, on the apparel shopping web site, this card-sorting technique can be used to group different types of apparel under specific categories.

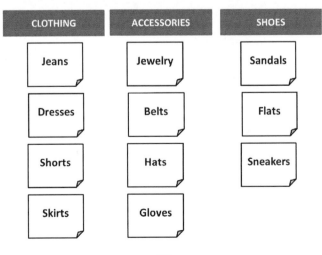

- Wireframes

Wireframes are used as a technique for designing UI layout. They are very helpful in deciding where each component such as navigation structures, content, image, and CTA should be placed on user interfaces.

Users usually don't read, but they scan the content. Thus user interfaces should be designed accordingly. At this stage design patterns such as F-shape should be used to increase the visibility of high-priority components (AOIs or areas of interest) on user interfaces.

Very High Priority Content	**High Priority Content**
High Priority Content	**Medium Priority Content**
Medium Priority Content	**Low Priority Content**

F. Interface Design

UX designers then convert interaction designs and information architectures into user interfaces by applying UX design and usability principles and guidelines (which are summarized at the first chapters of this book).

They design low-fidelity prototypes by sketching or using prototyping tools.

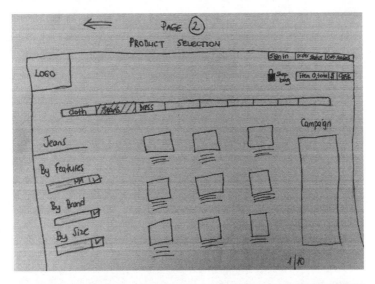

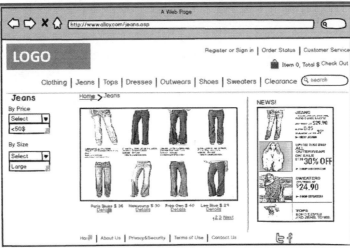

During low-fidelity prototyping, UX designers and business analysts may hesitate as to whether to behave like a craftsman or an artist. Until the Renaissance, the majority of architects designed their artifacts with a craftsman approach. Aesthetics was still very important for architects, but their main concern was designing buildings, bridges, and fountains that best met the needs of the public. After the freedom and creativity impact of the Renaissance, architects started to behave more like artists and focused on designing more aesthetic pieces.

Instead of trying to create Picasso-perfect designs with an artistic approach, business analysts and UX designers should always behave like craftsmen during low-fidelity prototyping. They should focus on meeting the functional needs of users in the most usable way, leaving aesthetic concerns to visual designers. In summary they should create low fidelity prototypes that mainly show how the product will interact with users without its visual "bells" and whistles".

G. Usability Testing

At this stage usability defects should be detected and resolved by usability testing of prototypes before they are sent to visual designers. This is the precondition of having a user-centered and iterative UX design process.

To increase the effectiveness and efficiency of usability tests, heuristic evaluations (against generally accepted usability criteria such as simplicity, consistency, error prevention, user control, efficiency of use, visibility, and language) should be made prior to user observations.

H. Visual Design

Visual designers convert low-fidelity prototypes into high-fidelity visual designs with the most aesthetic color, metaphor, and font selections.

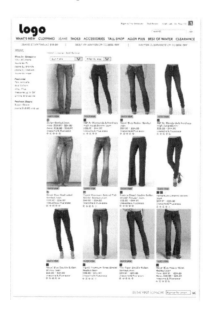

UX designers should be in collaboration with visual designers to ensure that visual designs are in alignment with low-fidelity prototypes and are not contradicting with usability principles.

This end-to-end, user-centered analysis and design methodology described in this section of the book helps to develop functional, usable, and visually aesthetic products.

9. Apply Usability Testing Techniques Such as Eye-Tracking

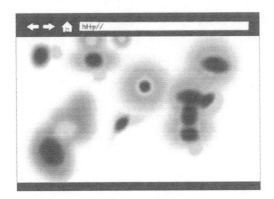

Usability is one of the nonfunctional requirements—such as performance, security, and reliability—that determine a product's quality level. It is the main indicator of how easily users can use a product.

Like other nonfunctional requirements, a product's usability should be also tested in every project. Project managers should not disregard usability testing efforts in their project plans.

Usability Testing Is Not Expensive

Sometimes project managers hesitate to allocate specific time and budget for usability testing, because they think a fully equipped test laboratory is mandatory to run usability tests.

However, rather than being a must-have, usability labs are a nice-to-have facility. Even inviting users to the project room and observing their interaction with interfaces can be enough to detect and analyze most usability problems.

Test Early

Unlike many other testing types such as performance, it is possible to test the usability of an incomplete product by using its prototype. This allows early defect detection and decreases the cost of usability problems.

Test with Real Users

Testing usability with a limited number of users who represent target personas is much better than testing with a lot of random users.

The optimum number of users that should be included in the tests is eight to ten per persona. For example, to test the usability of the apparel shopping web site with two personas, a total of twenty users will be more than enough.

Finding users representing target personas is one of the most challenging parts of usability tests. The user database of the company should be queried in an intelligent way to find users who represent persona groups. Before inviting people they should be phone-interviewed, and their social media profiles should be analyzed to check whether they really represent the personas or not.

Project team members' friends and family who represent personas are also good candidates for test participants. They can be easily reached and quickly invited to usability tests.

Eye-Tracking

At usability tests with user observation method, participants evaluate their experience on UI during the test (think aloud) or after the test session (retrospective protocols).

In either case, users may not provide fully complete, clear, and objective feedback about the usability of the product. Some of users even don't want to criticize the product, and they hesitate to make negative comments.

To mitigate this risk, a complementary test technique called eye-tracking can be utilized.

This technique makes it possible to detect the parts of user interfaces where users look while conducting the given tasks during the tests. This is done by tracking and recording their eye movements with a special eye-tracking tool. Detailed reports such as heat maps and gaze plots can be generated by the eye-tracking tool.

Although these reports don't tell what the user thought during his or her experience, the reports do make it possible to analyze

- where users focused most (heat maps),

- in which order they looked at each part of the user interface (gaze plots), and

- how long they stared at each part while completing the tasks.

Eye-tracking results should be combined with users' think-aloud and retrospective evaluations to identify usability defects.

Benchmarking: Don't Copy Your Competitors' Mistakes

Benchmarking user interfaces of a company's products with the competitors' is an alternative way of evaluating potential UX and usability issues. However even the best competitors don't always do the right things. Thus benchmarking should not result in copying competitors' mistakes. To mitigate this risk, benchmarking results should be supported with heuristic inspections that evaluate the usability of product against criteria such as consistency, error prevention, user control, efficiency, effectiveness, and visibility.

In one of the recent UXservices projects, our team was responsible for benchmarking the customer interaction channels of a global hotel chain with its competitors. During the study our team noticed that the majority of competitors had common good things and common wrong things on their customer-interaction channels (web, call center, mobile, and social media). This was a result of a copy-and-paste approach. Although copying good sides of competitors is a fast and effective way to make improvements, companies should also focus on finding ways to differentiate themselves in providing the best customer experience.

Interviews vs. Focus-Group Sessions

Since most products are used individually, one-to-one interviews are more effective than focus-group sessions to evaluate a product's usability. People usually impact each other's opinion during focus-group evaluations, and this may deteriorate the test results.

However, focus groups may be more advantageous compared to interviews, in case solution alternatives for usability problems are also brainstormed during the sessions.

Crowdsourcing

Crowdsourcing is another way of testing a product's usability. It is conducting tests with many remote users. Although crowdsourcing increases the size of the user base, the limited demographics structure of the user base is its main disadvantage. Most of the users in crowdsourcing communities are students and home workers, and they may not fully represent the personas of the products. Thus crowdsourcing test results should be supported with focus group, interview, and other classic usability test methods.

Customer Journey Mapping

Customer journey mapping is an effective tool to visualize and evaluate the end-to-end experience of customers at different touch points. From their own perspective, customers' experience, emotions, and satisfaction level at each part of the journey can be visualized on these maps.

In one of UXservices projects, the client was a utility services company that interacted with its customers on various interaction channels. Customers could search for service details and apply for subscription on the web page, complete the subscription at a dealer by signing a contract, get their invoices via e-mail, and make inquiries via the call center. Our UXservices team used a customer journey mapping technique to evaluate customers' end-to-end experience. In addition to finding improvement areas for each existing interaction channel, this study also determined the need for a mobile channel. Use cases for this new channel were also defined based on the details of the customer journey map. A summary of the customer journey map is shown below:

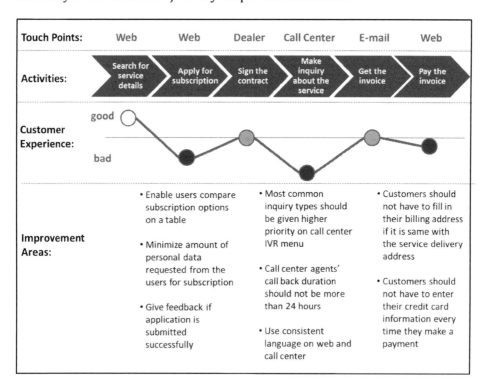

Adapt Global Testing Principles

Usability testing is a type of nonfunctional testing. Thus standard testing principles defined by global testing organizations such as ISTQB® (International Software Testing Qualifications Board) are also applicable for usability tests:

- Testing shows presence of defects

Testing shows the presence of defects but cannot prove zero defects.

Usability testing efforts reduce the number of undiscovered defects on the product but cannot claim zero defects.

- Exhaustive testing is impossible

Testing every part of a product is not possible, especially for fast-track projects, due to time and resource limitations. Instead of doing exhaustive testing, usability testing efforts should focus on areas with a high level of risk. Risk prioritization should be done according to potential impact and likelihood level.

- Early testing:

Testing should start as early as possible during the product development life cycle. Without waiting for the development of final product, usability testing should be started on prototypes. Even low-fidelity prototypes such as sketches can be used for early testing.

- Testing should be done differently in different context

Usability testing techniques may differ for different kinds of products. They may even differ in testing different parts of the same product. For example, in a recent project, our UXservices team was responsible for usability testing of a bank's web channel. Our team used eye-tracking technique in this project.

For usability testing of the home page, the team utilized heat-map analysis to measure the effectiveness of carousel area and other AOIs in attracting customers' attention on displayed product campaigns such as mortgage loans with low interest rates.

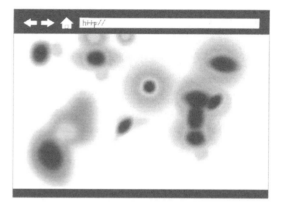

Whereas in usability testing of inner task-intensive pages such as money transfer, deposits, and credit cards, the team utilized gaze plot analysis. This technique showed in which sequence customers' eyes moved on different parts of a user interface. In this way the team identified usability problems regarding UI layout and navigation structures.

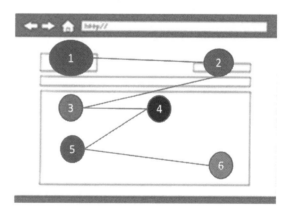

- Pesticide paradox

If the same kinds of tests are repeated again and again, the same set of test cases will no longer be able to find any new defects on the product. To overcome this "pesticide paradox," the test cases should be regularly reviewed and updated.

Products are like living organisms. Over months and years, many changes are done on these products. Additionally personas of these products and their mental model may also change in time.

Thus usability testing should not be regarded as a one-time activity that is conducted only at the product development stage. The usability of a product should be tested periodically after its release to ensure that it is always in perfect synchronization with its users.

To prevent pesticide paradox, the UX design team should review and update

- user profiles,

- personas,

- test cases (task scenarios), and

- usability test techniques

prior to each periodical usability test.

10. Show Return on Investment of Usability Studies

In most companies, usability tests are limited only to customer-facing products, because the usability problems on these products have a direct impact on sales, customer satisfaction, loyalty, and the company's profitability. The ROI (return on investment) of the usability studies on these products are usually very high and impressive.

This fact makes usability testing of customer-facing products the top priority for UX design teams.

Compared to customer-facing products, UX designers may have difficulty showing the value of usability tests on enterprise company products that are used by employees.

However, UX design teams should not undermine the value of usability tests on these products. The usability defects on enterprise products result in huge amounts of efficiency/productivity losses. Thus usability studies on these products can also generate very high cost-savings.

In one of UXservices' projects, our team's main focus was testing the usability of user interfaces at a telecommunications company's call center.

Before and after the usability study, the team measured KPIs (key performance indicators) regarding efficiency. Then these figures were compared to measure the outcome of usability improvements. The ROI was calculated as follows:

- 900 call center agents used the call center application.

- Hourly labor rate of a user was $10.

- Number of transactions per user per day was 40.

- The budget of usability study was $40,000 (cost of usability study + development efforts to fix the defects).

- The usability improvements saved an average of 0.2 minutes per user/transaction.

So in total, the usability study had the following results:

- A total efficiency improvement of 900 x 40 x 0.2 = 7,200 minutes = 120 hours per day was achieved.

- With a labor cost of $10/hour, this improvement corresponded to a saving of $1,200/day = $ 1,200 x 365= $438,000 per year.

- This resulted in $438,000 saving / $40,000 cost = 1.095% return on investment.

After presenting this very high ROI, the company's management team recognized the importance of usability studies, even on the productivity of employees.

11. Benefit from Requirements Management, Prototyping, and Usability Testing Tools

The efficiency and effectiveness of requirements analysis, UX design, and usability testing processes can be improved by using

- requirements management,

- prototyping, and

- usability-testing tools.

Requirements Management Tools

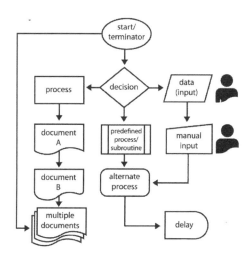

Requirements-management tools guide project team members in documenting and tracking requirements. Requirements are automatically stored in the repository of these tools to enable end-to-end traceability throughout the product-development life cycle. Every update of the requirements analysis, UX design, and test artifacts can be tracked by the configuration-management capability of the tools. Functional and usability test scenarios can be easily prepared by importing the requirements from the analysis module. Defects found after each test run can then be associated with the relevant test cases and requirements.

The new generation of requirements management tools also provides a collaborative platform for the project team with a Facebook-like communication architecture.

On these tools project team members at discrete locations can work in the same virtual workplace. In this virtual workplace, project team members are represented virtually, and their work is published as status updates. They can work together on the same requirement documents and prototypes. They are notified for every change on requirements, prototypes, and test cases by advanced configuration management features. This virtual collaboration makes it possible to apply agile methodologies in development of products by distributed teams at discrete locations.

Prototyping Tools

Prototyping tools allow mocking up the products and simulating them by using a rich widget library.

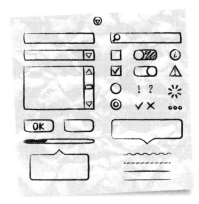

Prototyping tools have features that allow interactive user actions such as navigating among user interfaces, selecting options by clicking on radio buttons, and getting notifications by error messages.

Thanks to these interactive features, both functionality- and usability-related defects can be easily found by users and fixed at the early phases of the project. Since the development of the product is not complete at this stage, change requests received on low-fidelity prototypes are not as painful and costly as they would be at later stages of development.

Sometimes graphic design tools are used by UX designers for low-fidelity prototyping, although these tools are not suitable for this task. Since the aim of graphic design tools is polishing user interfaces, they may mislead the team and shift their focus from functional and usability aspects to visual details such as colors and font types. As mentioned in previous chapters, designing visually aesthetic high-fidelity prototypes is the responsibility of visual designers.

Usability Testing Tools

There are two main types of usability testing tools. These are logging and eye-tracking tools. Although these tools are not a must-have for usability tests, they are very useful in recording and analyzing user observation sessions.

As explained in previous chapters, eye-tracking tools allow tracking and recording users' eye movements. In this way they make it possible to analyze where users mostly focused on user interfaces and in what order.

Logging tools enable recording users' faces, voices, and their interactions on the screens at the same time.

By analyzing the records of eye-tracking and logging tools, we can detect usability defects. Also, without a need for a stopwatch and detailed session notes, they allow to measure key usability metrics, such as

- how long users spent on each task,

- how many users could complete the given tasks,

- how many times the user was misled by user interfaces and had to navigate back,

- how much time users spent to recover from errors, and

- how many times the help menus were used.

In addition to these quantitative metrics, qualitative metrics such as user satisfaction level can be generated on these tools by conducting surveys automatically before, during, and after the test sessions.

In this way we can measure the quality level of user interfaces in terms of key usability criteria such as efficiency, effectiveness, error tolerance, satisfaction, and easiness to learn.

Mitigate Tool-Related Risks

With all their benefits, tools also bring some new risks in the product development life cycle. To fully benefit from tools, the following risks should be mitigated:

1. Formulating a wrong-automation strategy

In recent years, we have started to see a different "ware" category than hardware and software. This category is called shelfware.

Shelfware represents the automation software that sits on the shelves of the company without being used by any single person.

Shelfware causes a huge amount of sunk cost for companies. In some public companies, high license and support costs paid for useless automation software have become an issue investigated during internal audits.

Some managers want to press a button and let the computer automatically do the majority of requirement analysis, UX design, and usability-testing work instead of utilizing people for these tasks. Unfortunately, this is only a management dream.

2. Positioning tools as magicians

Automation tools have limits. They can help the project team do their work in a more convenient way by automating only some of their tasks, not all of them.

If the maturity of an organization's requirements analysis, UX design, and usability testing processes is at a good level, automation makes it better; otherwise, automation may even make it worse.

Hence managers should first focus on improving their teams' user-centered analysis, UX design, and usability testing skills and then give the start for the automation initiative.

If the team has no knowledge of basic techniques such as requirements gathering, use cases, user profiling, persona definitions, prototyping, and user observation, then automation will bring only extra problems rather than benefits. This will accelerate the chaos within the organization.

An iterative approach of first implementing these techniques by using simple templates and then adapting the automation tools is the best-proven way of success.

3. Starting to implement a tool at the wrong time

On the other side, automation is a challenging project itself. The time needed to implement automation tools should be considered as a separate risk item in every project.

An automation tool should not be used for the first time in a time-sensitive, high-priority project. The team should focus on the project itself instead of allocating their limited time for tool implementation.

They should remember that upper management always takes into account the score but not how the team played during the game.

12. Adapt a User-Centered Approach in Waterfall and Agile Projects

There are two popular product development methodologies: One of them is classical "waterfall" methodology and the other one is "agile".

Which One Is Better: Waterfall or Agile?

Since "agile" has a similar meaning to "quick," which is one of the most nice-to-hear words in product development, agile became very popular in a short time.

In popular agile framework, Scrum, there is no need for detailed requirement documents and prototypes with long annotations.

Requirements are defined as short and simple user stories (as a "role," I want "goal") on the product backlog by a client representative called the product owner. An agile team (consists of developers and testers) releases a working part of the product in a series of weeks-long "sprints" under the coordination of a "Scrum master."

One of the agile manifesto statements is "customer collaboration over contract negotiation." Agile removes the "checks and balances" within the project team and brings a *leaner product development life cycle*. The product owner and the development team work at the same location, which creates a more user-centered and collaborative product-development environment.

Agile projects' fast delivery of working products starting from the first iteration brings confidence to all stakeholders.

However, at waterfall projects development waits for the completion of whole product's analysis and design phases, and it takes a long time to start getting the working parts of the product. Clients usually first see user interfaces at the UAT (user acceptance test), which is the final phase of the project. However, even the most experienced project teams can't produce the optimum design at the first trial. Good design is a result of several iterations. Iteration is even the secret behind development of everything in life. All the complex systems that surround us once started as a simple system and evolved in an iterative and progressive way. Iteration is a cycle of doing something, testing it, improving it, and retesting it. Making iterations on the final product by adapting CRs is a very costly approach, since after each iteration the majority of a product's components have to be changed and retested. This latency in product delivery at waterfall projects and creates anxiety on clients who are impatient to see "quick" results.

Agile Is Not Always the Best Choice

Despite all its advantages compared to waterfall, there are some difficulties in realizing agile's theoretical framework.

Applying agile methodology to every kind of project is not a correct strategy, especially for the development of products that have intensive integration among their components. If agile is applied in these kinds of projects, the following happens: The team delivers product parts A and B without any major problems at the first iterations. Nevertheless, the team realizes that they have to make changes to parts A and B while working on part C, since it has integration points with those parts. In other words, A and B have to be refactored, although they have already been released. Refactoring means changing the internal structure of a product without changing its behavior, and it is always harder than developing from scratch. These back-and-forth moves with challenging refactoring efforts make the build and delivery of the product with many integrated parts even more difficult at later iterations, making waterfall a better alternative.

The other challenge of applying agile methodology is keeping all team members at the same location. This is almost impossible, since in most companies, people usually work at different locations simultaneously for many different projects.

A Hybrid Approach

During development of products with many integrated components by many people at diverse locations, the best strategy is applying a hybrid approach that integrates agile's *lean, iterative, and user-centered* structure with waterfall.

This can be achieved by benefiting from *prototyping* throughout the whole project, rather than using it only during the user interface design phase. Prototyping enables getting early feedback from users in a more iterative way throughout the project, starting from requirements-gathering meetings until the end of development phase.

The project team and the client should frequently come together and evaluate the functionality and usability of product, with low-fidelity prototypes even created with sketching. Changing the prototypes will always be much easier and faster compared to changing the completed product. By this iterative and user-centered approach, a high number of CRs coming from clients can be prevented. Also early detection of defects and CRs without waiting for late user-acceptance tests reduces their fixing cost.

Prototyping Has Its Own Risks

Although it adds more iterative and user-centered attributes to waterfall projects, prototyping introduces some new risks that have to be mitigated.

One of these risks concerns clients. Clients think that a product is composed of only user interfaces. They usually have no idea about technical components of the product. The first time they see the interactive prototypes created on the tools, which may be difficult to distinguish from the real product, they think that the product itself is ready for release. When they hear that the prototype is only a mock-up and the release will be five months later, they feel disappointed. They accuse the project team of delaying them unnecessarily by not delivering a product that is ready to go live. To mitigate this risk, clients should be informed in advance about the purpose of prototyping.

The other risk about prototyping concerns developers. Developers usually don't like to read requirements documents prepared by business analysts. They prefer to start developing the product as soon as they get the preliminary versions of prototypes. Project managers should prevent this situation and ensure that the development waits until the requirements documents are reviewed and signed off by clients. Otherwise, it is hard to keep the product updated with changes on requirement documents and user interfaces.

13. Apply Change Management in Deployment of the New, User-Centered Methodology

For companies, the requirements analysis and UX design methodology they apply during PDLC (product development lifecycle) has a similar role to the DNA of living beings.

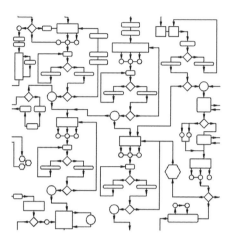

DNA is the enabler of self-organization in cellular structure. If the body has a good DNA, it is healthy; otherwise it suffers from diseases.

Similarly the existence of structural problems in requirements analysis and UX design methodology guarantees only the development of failing products rather than successful ones.

"Insanity Is Doing the Same Things Over And Over Again and Expecting Different Results" Albert Einstein

After repeatedly failing to produce successful products, most companies transform their requirements analysis and UX design methodology to a more user-centered one.

Revolutionary or Evolutionary

There are two alternative ways of implementing a new methodology: revolutionary or evolutionary.

In the revolutionary approach, the new requirements analysis and UX design roles, principles, tools, and techniques start to be used as a whole just after the kickoff, whereas in the evolutionary approach they are applied as milestones in an iterative way.

The "forming, storming, norming, and performing" model of group development that Bruce Tuckman proposed is also applicable when implementing a new methodology. All of these four consequent phases are necessary for an organization to face up to challenges, resolve them, and start to deliver best results.

Hence, it is wiser to implement evolutionarily rather than revolutionarily, especially in transition to a new, user-centered requirements analysis and UX design methodology at large-scale companies.

Rome Was Not Built in a Day

Managers should have vision and ambition for a successful transformation. They should also be patient during implementation of the new methodology.

They should remember that it is not the strength of waves that shapes the rocks, but it is their persistence. Thus they should continuously implement change-management principles to manage internal resistance without giving up.

They should act as role models and involve all relevant stakeholders in the reengineering process to increase their ownership.

Change Agents

Managers should ensure that all stakeholders in the organization have the awareness and understanding of the new user-centered requirements analysis and UX design methodology.

Among all of these people, business analysts and UX designers have the most important role in this transformation.

They should act as change agents who motivate the use of new principles, tools, and techniques by all relevant stakeholders. They should also act as thought leaders in building and penetrating the requirements analysis and UX design knowhow in their organization.

Designing User Experience Is Like Cooking

In addition to beginning with a good recipe, every delicious food requires the desire and passion of the person cooking it.

Similarly methodologies are not enough to ensure great user experience. The other most important factor is the desire and passion of business analysts and UX designers about user-centricity.

Index

user researcher 10

user story 86

user task analysis 47

UX design guidelines 20

UX design principles 14,20

UX designer 10,11,24,28,31,32,33,34,

25,36,38,47,48,62,63,76,81,93

V

viral impact 58

vision and scope document 39

visual designer 10,29,62,63,81

W

waterfall 85,86,87,88

web services 36

wireframe 60

workshop 29

Made in the USA
Lexington, KY
23 September 2015